SCHOLASTIC
PHONICS
CLUBHOUSE ™

Workbook

10

John Shefelbine

California State University at Sacramento
Story Editor

1 2 3 4 5 6 7 8 9 10   14   04 03 02 01 00 99 98 97

Contents

Workbook 10

Welcome!

LISTEN AND WRITE

b**r**oom
g**r**een
tree

Look at each picture. Write the letters that stand for the first two sounds in the picture name.

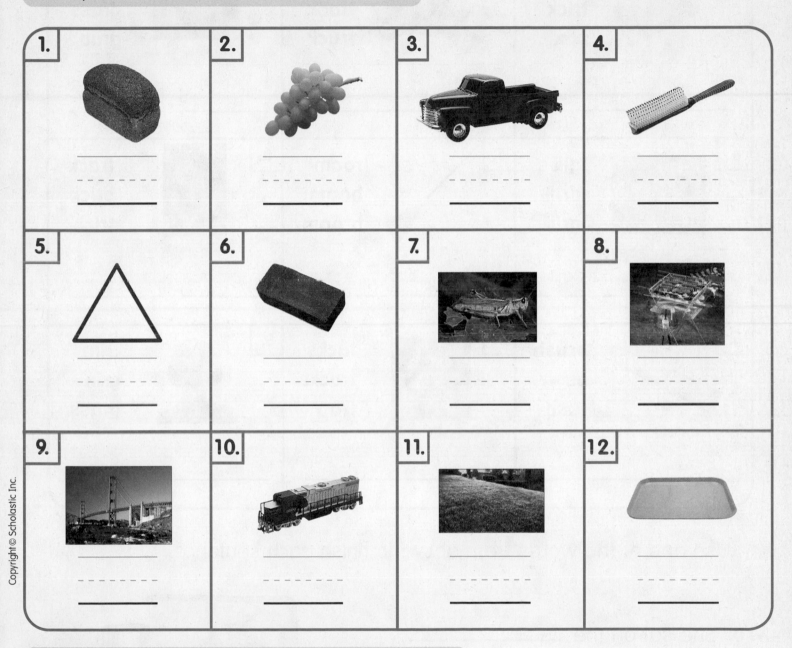

1.

_____
- - - - - - - - - - -
_____

2.

_____
- - - - - - - - - - -
_____

3.

_____
- - - - - - - - - - -
_____

4.

_____
- - - - - - - - - - -
_____

5.

_____
- - - - - - - - - - -
_____

6.

_____
- - - - - - - - - - -
_____

7.

_____
- - - - - - - - - - -
_____

8.

_____
- - - - - - - - - - -
_____

9.

_____
- - - - - - - - - - -
_____

10.

_____
- - - - - - - - - - -
_____

11.

_____
- - - - - - - - - - -
_____

12.

_____
- - - - - - - - - - -
_____

Write the letters **br**, **gr**, or **tr** to finish each word. Read the words to a friend.

13. ____uck   14. ____ab   15. ____ick

Recognize *r*-Blends   **3**

Circle the word that names each picture.
Then write the word on the line.

1.
brick
trick
box
_____

2.
tuck
track
truck
_____

3.
gas
grass
grab
_____

4.
gill
drill
grill
_____

5.
room
boom
broom
_____

6.
track
brick
trick
_____

7.
brush
bush
rush
_____

8.
tacks
tracks
trap
_____

9.
trim
grin
grass
_____

Use one of the words from above to finish each sentence.

10. She sat on the _____.

11. A big _____ went past.

Look at each picture. Write the letters that stand for the first two sounds in the picture name.

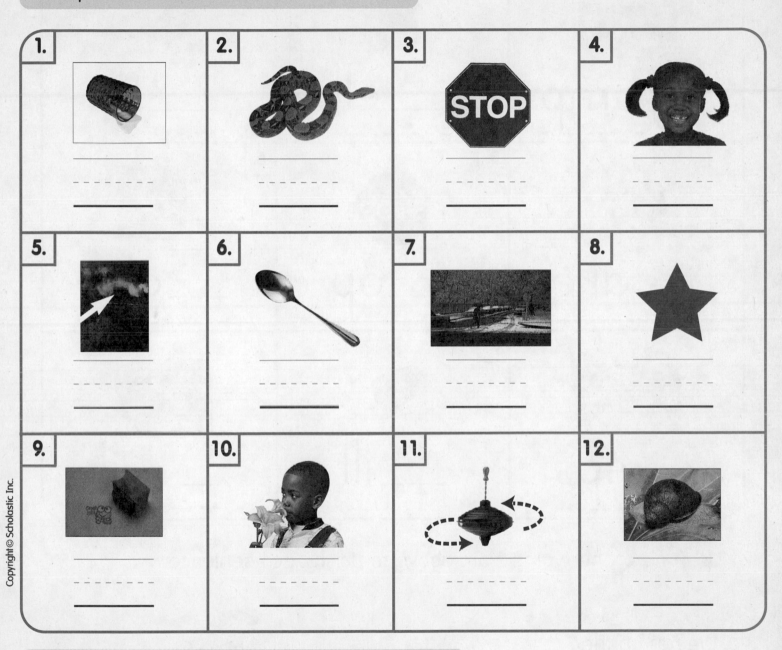

1.

2.

3.

4.

5.

6.

7.

8.

9.

10.

11.

12.

Write the letters **sm**, **sn**, **sp**, or **st** to finish each word. Read the words to a friend.

13. _____ell   14. _____ack   15. _____in

Look at each picture. Write the missing letters to finish the picture name.

1.
__ __ amp

2.
__ __ ell

3.
__ __ in

4.
__ __ ake

5.
__ __ op

6.
__ __ oke

7.
__ __ eps

8.
__ __ ill

9.
__ __ ail

Use one of the words from above to finish each sentence.

10. We ran up the __ __ __ __ __ __ __ __ __ __ .

11. Mom said we had to __ __ __ __ __ __ __ __ __ __ .

Add the letter or letters to the word part below it. Blend the word. If it is a real word, write it on the line.

f r k v
w j s

___ ing

1. _____

2. _____

3. _____

4. _____

g h br st
m th sw

___ ing

5. _____

6. _____

7. _____

8. _____

Write a sentence using two of the words you made.

9. _____

_____

_____

Use the letter tiles to make words.

a	st	e	o	p

1. st ___ ___ p

2. ___ ___ ___ ___

3. ___ ___ ___ ___

n	sp	sk	i	d

4. sp ___ ___ n

5. ___ ___ ___ ___

6. ___ ___ ___ ___

p	tr	sk	i	a

7. tr ___ ___ ___

8. ___ ___ ___ ___

9. ___ ___ ___

tr	u	b	ck	t

10. tr ___ ck

11. ___ ___ ___ ___

12. ___ ___ ___ ___

cheese
shark

Look at each picture. Write the two letters that stand for the first sound in the picture name.

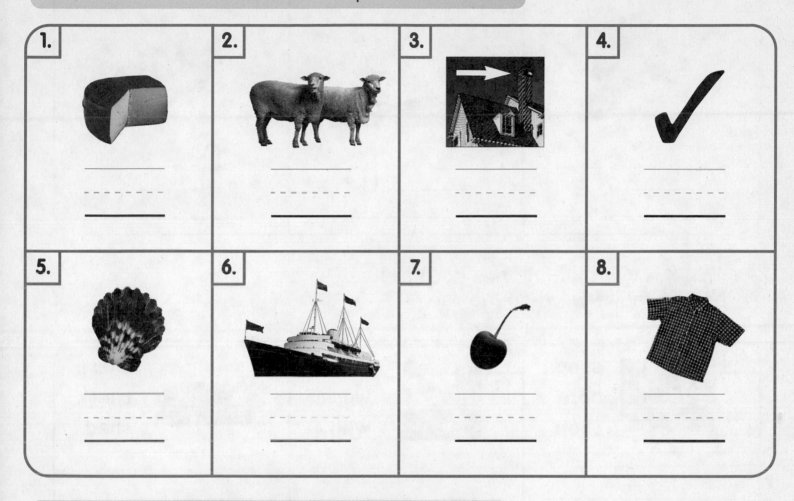

1.	2.	3.	4.
_____	_____	_____	_____

5.	6.	7.	8.
_____	_____	_____	_____

Look at each picture. Write the two letters that stand for the last sound in the picture name.

9.	10.	11.	12.
_____	_____	_____	_____

Recognize Digraphs /ch/ch, /sh/sh   9

Look at each picture. Write the missing letters to finish the picture name.

1. _____ in

2. _____ ip

3. fi _____

Circle the word that names each picture. Then write the word on the line.

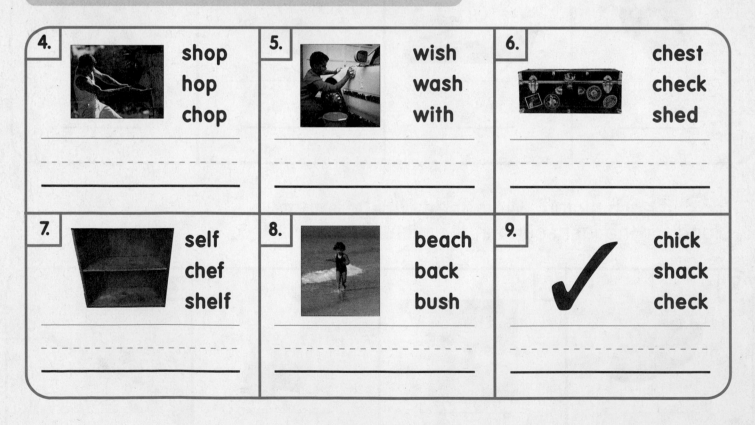

4. shop
hop
chop

5. wish
wash
with

6. chest
check
shed

7. self
chef
shelf

8. beach
back
bush

9. chick
shack
check

~Trust Me~

The duck was stuck in a trap.

"I can get a good price for you at the shop, duck," said the man.

"Set me free, and make a wish," said the duck. "I will make your wish come true. You can be rich. You can live like a king."

"Is this a trick?" the man asked.

"Just trust me," said the duck.

"This was a trick!" the man said.

"But you got your wish," said the duck.

"You got your big fish! I can't help it if you let it go."

Swish, swish! The duck and the fish swam off.

Circle the words in the story that begin with **tr**. Underline the words that rhyme with **sing**.

The man was hungry. "I wish I had a big fish for lunch," he said. So the man and the duck went to the pond.

"Stand still on this spot," said the duck. "I will bring you a big fish."

"Is this a trick?" the man asked.

"Just trust me," said the duck.

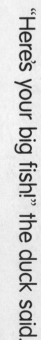

"Here's your big fish!" the duck said. The man grabbed for the fish. Swish, swish! The fish smacked him in the chest. Swish, swish! The fish smashed him on the chin.

"Stop!" cried the man, as he dropped the fish back into the pond.

thumb
the
w<u>h</u>eel

Look at each picture. Write the two letters that stand for the first sound in the picture name.

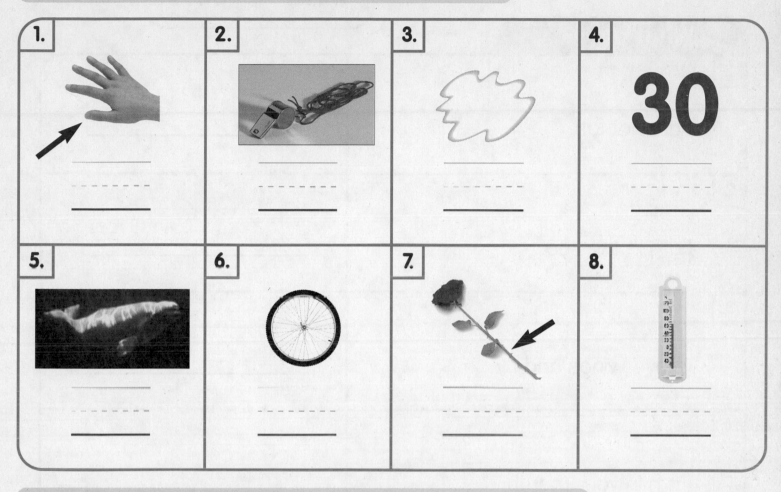

1.

2.

3.

4.

30

5.

6.

7.

8.

Look at each picture. If the picture name begins with the **th** sound as in **thumb**, write **th** on the first line. If it ends with **th** as in **path**, write **th** on the second line.

9.

10.

13

11.

12.

Recognize Digraphs /th/th, /hw/wh 13

Choose a word from the box to answer each riddle. Then write the word on the line.

tooth	moth
white	thin
wheel	whale

What am I?

1. I am not fat.

2. I am in the sea.

3. I have wings and fly.

4. I am in your mouth.

5. I am on a bike.

6. I am a color.

Look at each picture. Write the letters that stand for the two sounds at the beginning of the picture name.

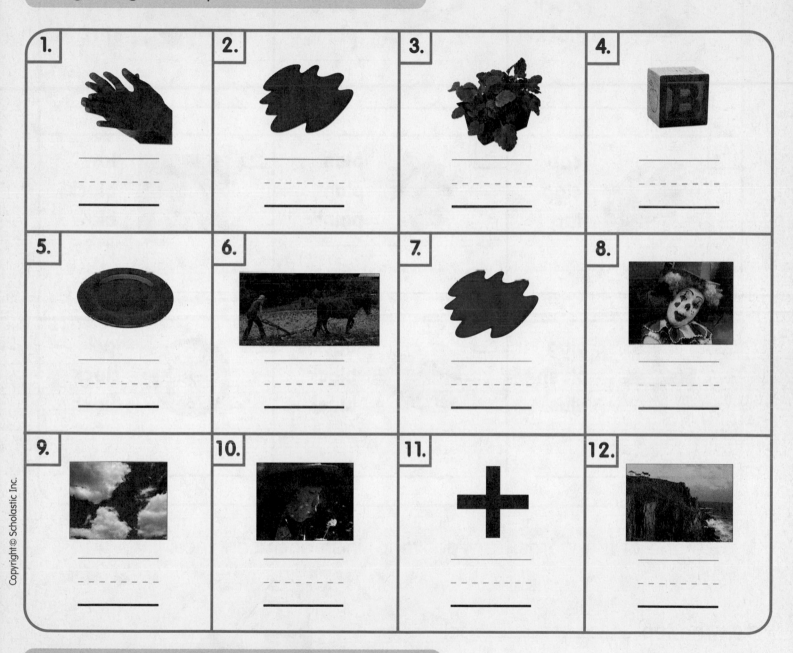

1.

2.

3.

4.

5.

6.

7.

8.

9.

10.

11.

12.

Write the letters **bl**, **cl**, or **pl** to finish each word. Read the words to a friend.

13. ____us

14. ____ub

15. ____ank

Circle the word that names each picture.
Then write the word on the line.

1.
block
clock
flock

_____

2.
lane
plate
plane

_____

3.
bluff
cliff
stiff

_____

4.
cap
clap
lap

_____

5.
plan
plant
paint

_____

6.
low
block
blow

_____

7.
plug
blush
plus

_____

8.
back
block
black

_____

9.
lock
clock
block

_____

Use one of the words from above to finish each sentence.

_____

10. The top _____ fell.

_____

11. It was _____, not red.

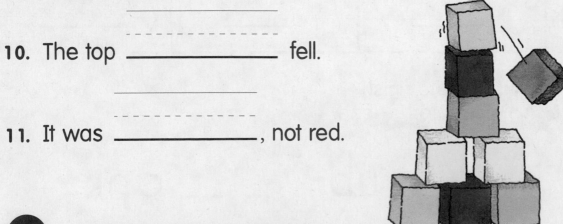

gate bone
nine cube

Look at each picture. Write the missing letters to finish the picture name.

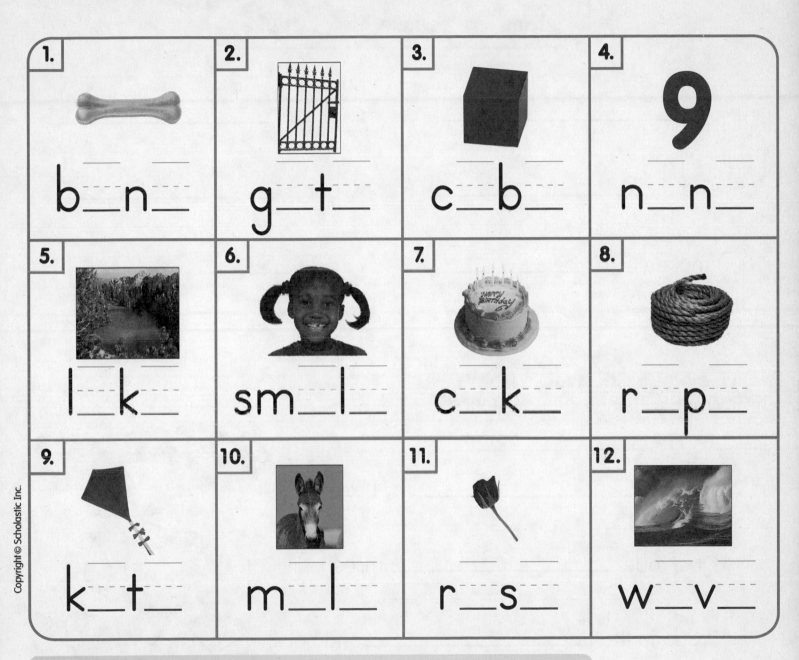

1. b_n_

2. g_t_

3. c_b_

4. n_n_

5. l_k

6. sm_l_

7. c_k_

8. r_p

9. k_t_

10. m_l_

11. r_s_

12. w_v_

Write the letters **a** and **e**, **i** and **e**, or **o** and **e**, to finish each word. Read the words to a friend.

13. h_d_

14. n_s_

15. r_k_

Choose a word from the box that rhymes with each word below. Then write the word on the line.

ride	five	fuse
stone	lake	spoke

1. use _____

2. shake _____

3. side _____

4. bone _____

5. smoke _____

6. dive _____

Use one of the words from above to finish each sentence.

7. I like to _____ my bike.

8. I just rode _____ miles!

9. I rode to the _____ and back.

10. I _____ to my friend at the lake.

Add the letter or letters to the word part below it.
Blend the word. If it is a real word, write it on the line.

b d c n
p sh t y

___ ake

1. _____

2. _____

3. _____

4. _____

c f h l
J n pl t

___ ane

5. _____

6. _____

7. _____

8. _____

Write a sentence using two of the words you made.

9. _____

Read the poem. Complete the sentences using words from the poem.

Where's My Lunch?

Where's my lunch?
  Bring it quick!
Make me some pancakes,
  Wide and thick!

Where's my lunch?
  Don't make me wait!
Shake them, bake them,
  Plop them on a plate!

Where's my lunch?
  Pile them in a stack!
Crunch, crunch, munch, munch!
  Bring fifty more back!

1. The pancakes are _____ and thick.

2. He likes to pile them in a _____.

Check each word as you read it to a partner.
Circle any words you need to practice.

I can read!

- ☐ drive
- ☐ cute
- ☐ glass
- ☐ sting
- ☐ hope

- ☐ path
- ☐ smile
- ☐ shape
- ☐ much
- ☐ white

- ☐ fish
- ☐ black
- ☐ chest
- ☐ thick
- ☐ plane

Lookout Words!

- ☐ where
- ☐ said
- ☐ my
- ☐ above
- ☐ don't
- ☐ more
- ☐ was
- ☐ what
- ☐ your
- ☐ here

Fill in the bubble next to the word that best finishes each sentence. Then write the word on the line.

1.	Mom and I went on a fine _____.	○ **trip** ○ **trap** ○ **grip**
2.	We didn't _____ my sister.	○ **shake** ○ **flake** ○ **take**
3.	We ate lunch on the _____.	○ **lane** ○ **plane** ○ **crane**
4.	We went to a big _____.	○ **branch** ○ **ranch** ○ **crunch**
5.	_____ we got home, we gave Dad a hug.	○ **When** ○ **Then** ○ **Hen**
6.	"What did you _____ me?" asked my sister.	○ **ring** ○ **string** ○ **bring**

Assess: Words With *r*-Blends, *s*-Blends, *l*-Blends; Digraphs; Final *e*

The Fox and the Grapes

Fox was hungry. "I must rush home," he said. "I must have lunch." Then something made him stop. Sniff, sniff, went Fox. "What is that I smell?" Sniff, sniff. "I smell ripe grapes!"

"I can't spend any more time here!" said Fox. "Those grapes aren't so good anyway. They may smell fine, but I think they're bad. I don't want them at all!"

MORAL: It is easy to dislike what you can't have.

Circle the words that begin with **sm** and **sn.** Underline the words that begin with **th.**

Fox opened the gate and went in. A bunch of ripe grapes hung from a thick vine. "I'll just snatch that bunch of grapes," Fox said with a grin. Snap, snap, went his mouth. Click, click, went his teeth. Fox tried and tried, but he could not reach the grapes.

Fox had a plan. He said, "I'll shake the vine. Then I'll pick up the grapes that fall!" Shake, shake, shake, went Fox. Swing, swing, swing, went the grapes. Fox tried and tried, but not one grape fell.

Circle the word that names each picture. Then write the word on the line.

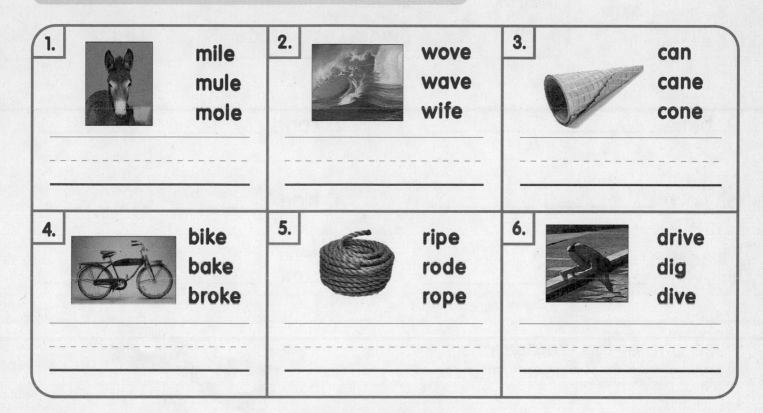

1. mile
mule
mole

2. wove
wave
wife

3. can
cane
cone

4. bike
bake
broke

5. ripe
rode
rope

6. drive
dig
dive

Write the word that names each picture.

7.

8.

Choose a word from the box that rhymes with each word below. Then write the word on the line.

> broke   shake   stone
> kite   plane   wide

1. bake _____

2. cone _____

3. poke _____

4. hide _____

5. white _____

6. cane _____

Use one of the words from above to finish each sentence.

7. He has a red and white _____.

8. It is in the shape of a _____.

9. It has very _____ wings.

10. His last kite flew away

    when the string _____ .

26 Blend and Write Words With Final *e*

Look at each picture. Write the letter that begins the picture name.

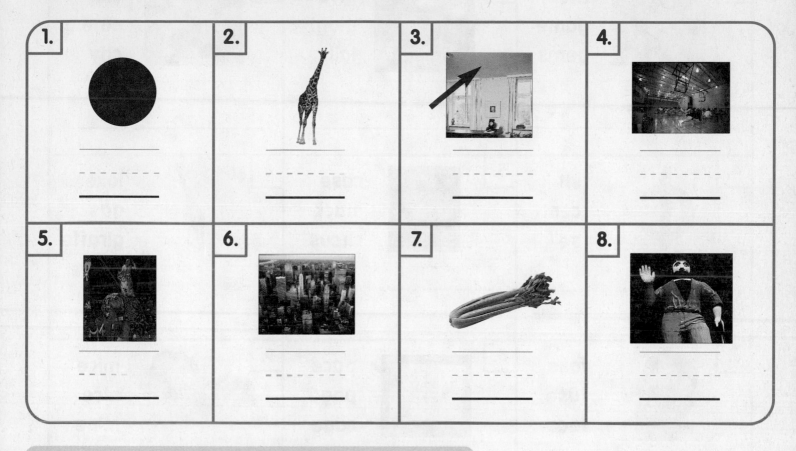

1.

2.

3.

4.

5.

6.

7.

8.

Write the letter **c** or **g** to finish each word. Circle the word that names the picture.

9. ___ent   10. ___ems

Remember, both **c** and **g** can stand for more than one sound.

Recognize /s/c, /j/g 27

Circle the word that names each picture.
Then write the word on the line.

1.
them
game
gems

2.
give
giant
jail

3.
clay
cute
city

4.
¢
sit
cent
sell

5.
case
stack
circus

6.
joke
gas
giraffe

7.
fake
fuse
face

8.
pace
page
cage

9.
mice
nice
mine

Use one of the words from
above to finish each sentence.

10. We saw a tall _____ in the zoo.

11. The zoo is in a big _____.

Blend and Write Words With /s/c, /j/g

Add the letter or letters to the word part below it. Blend the word. If it is a real word, write it on the line.

n   ch   m
fr   d

___ ice

1. _____

2. _____

3. _____

b   pr   r
sl   th

___ ice

4. _____

5. _____

6. _____

Write a sentence using two of the words you made.

7. _____

_____

_____

Finish each word ladder. Change only one letter at a time.

1. Go from ship to clap.

2. Go from five to nice.

3. Go from wish to list.

4. Go from rope to poke.

MUSH ON!

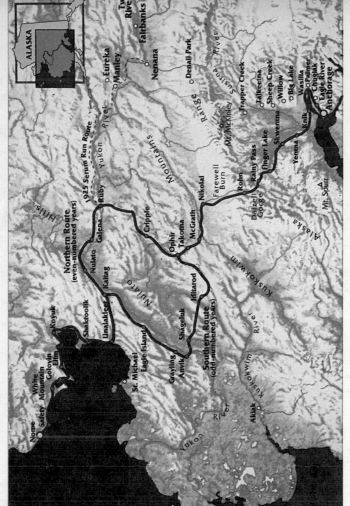

Alaska is a cold, cold place. It has lots of ice and snow. A sled dog race is held there. It is a huge race. The race is more than 1,000 miles long!

The people who drive the sleds are called mushers. Do you know why? To get the dogs to start the race, they yell, "Mush!"

This is the end of the race. Here comes the musher who will win! What a thrill! The best musher wins a huge prize. What a smile the musher has on her face!

Circle the words in the story that rhyme with **mice**. Underline the words that rhyme with **face**.

2

This race is hard to win. Many things can happen. Ice can crack. A sled can smash. A musher can slip and fall. The cold winds blast the sleds. The dogs are strong, but they can get sick. Some sleds won't make it to the end.

The mushers stop to rest. The dogs must eat and rest, too. Mushers make a nice resting place for them. Vets check the dogs. Then it's time to mush on!